LONELY QATAR TRAVEL GUIDE

Experience The Rich Culture And History Of Qatar Through Travel

Billie Schwartz

Table Of Contents:

Map Of Doha

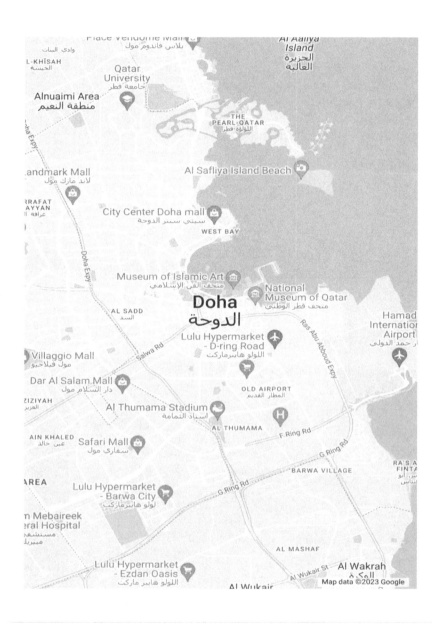

Map Of Al Khor

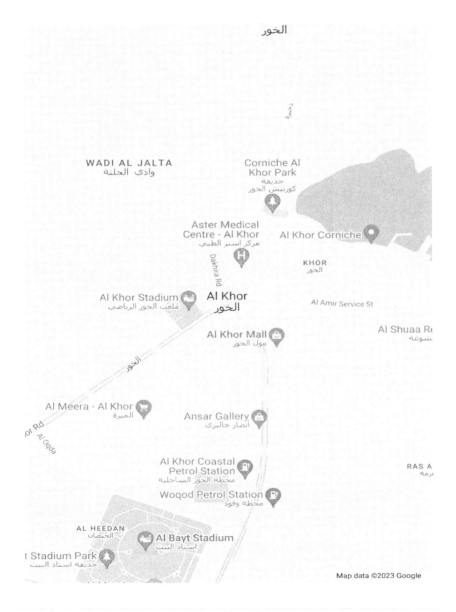

Map Of Al Wakrah

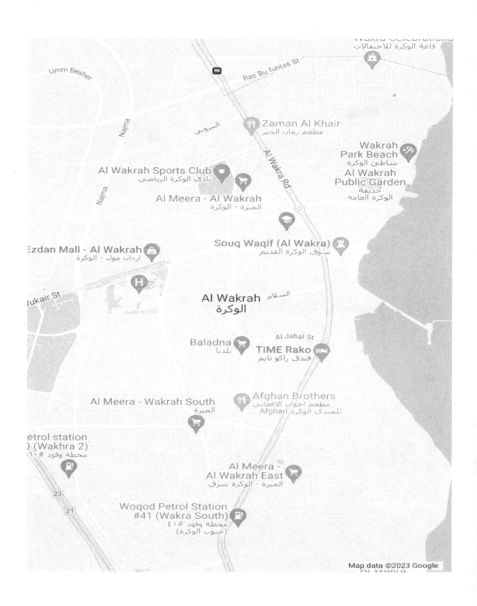

Map Of Al Rayyan

Introduction

We're glad you're here at Lonely Planet Qatar! A little, oil-rich nation in the Middle East called Qatar is a fantastic destination. Qatar gives visitors a memorable experience with its breathtaking desert vistas, energetic cities, and rich culture. Everyone may find something to enjoy in Qatar, from striking dunes and oases to contemporary skyscrapers.

You can discover all the information you need to plan a successful trip to Qatar in our travel guide. The information in this book will help you get the most out of your vacation, from the finest places to eat and stay to advice on how to navigate the nation and what to do.

Whether you're a seasoned tourist or a first-timer, this book will assist you in appreciating Qatar's natural beauty and rich cultural heritage. Prepare yourself to discover Qatar and create some priceless experiences!

CHAPTER ONE

About Qatar

History

Qatar is a tiny yet powerful country situated in the Persian Gulf. It has an incredibly lengthy and fascinating history, dating back to ancient times. Today, Qatar is a major regional power, with a rapidly-growing economy and strong ties to the global economy. It is also a major political player in the Middle East, particularly in the aftermath of the Arab Spring uprisings.

Qatar has been inhabited since at least the 4th millennium BC, and it is believed that the region was first settled by nomadic tribes from the Arabian Peninsula. During the ages, the area was dominated by different regional powers, including the Assyrians, Babylonians, and Persians. In the 15th century, Qatar fell under the dominion of the Ottoman Empire, which maintained dominance until the beginning of the 20th century, when it became a British protectorate.

In 1971, Qatar declared its independence and adopted a new constitution. Qatar has witnessed exceptional economic progress since then, thanks partly to its massive oil and gas reserves. It has become a major hub for international business, hosting the headquarters of many multinational corporations.

Qatar is also a major player in the Middle Eastern political scene, having recently opened its doors to the Arab Spring uprisings.

It has taken a strong stance on the situation in Syria and has been a significant backer of the Syrian opposition, offering financial and diplomatic assistance. Furthermore, by hosting a number of summits and conferences, Qatar has played an important role in global diplomacy.

Qatar is also home to a rich cultural legacy, with numerous traditional festivals and events, such as the yearly Qatar National Day festivities. Doha is also home to the largest museum in the Middle East, the Qatar National Museum, which shows a multitude of antiques and artwork.

Qatar is a highly vibrant nation, with a rich and intriguing past. From its ancient roots to its current role in the international political scene, Qatar has played an important role in shaping the region and the world.

Culture

The sovereign state of Qatar is located in the Arabian Peninsula's Qatar Peninsula, in the Middle East. The Persian Gulf, Saudi Arabia, and Bahrain border it on the east, south, and west, respectively. Qatar's art, music, cuisine, and architecture have all been influenced by the region's diverse cultural heritage, which includes influences from South Asia, the Middle East, Africa, and the Middle East.

The culture of Qatar is a mix of traditional Islamic and Arabic elements, which have been merged with influences from other nations and civilizations. Although Arabic is the official language of Qatar, English is widely spoken and understood, particularly in the capital city of Doha. Although traditional Qatari attire varies by location, it often consists of a long white robe, a headscarf, a curved dagger or sword for males, and a long white robe, all of which are worn by both sexes.

Qatari cuisine combines flavors from India and the Middle East unusually. 'Chebab,' a type of pancake made with flour, eggs, and spices, and machbous,' a type of rice dish, are popular dishes. Traditional sweets in Qatar include 'balaleet,' a sweet pastry dish, and 'halwa,' a sort of sweet prepared with crushed sesame seeds, almonds, and spices.

Qatar's music scene is thriving, with traditional Arabian and Indian sounds, as well as more modern genres such as Hip-

Hop, R&B, and Pop, playing important roles. Traditional Qatari instruments include the oud, a type of lute, and the tablah, a type of drum.

Qatar has a plethora of museums and galleries that showcase the country's extensive cultural heritage. Popular attractions include the Qatar National Museum, which features exhibits of artifacts from the country's past, and the Museum of Islamic Art, which houses a wide range of Islamic art and artifacts.

In Qatari art, traditional Islamic and Arabic components are vibrantly combined with more modern forms. Calligraphy, painting, sculpture, and photography are examples of popular art genres.

Qatar is an enthralling nation with a diverse cultural past. Qatar is a nation with something for everyone to discover and enjoy, from its traditional attire and food to its growing music scene and art.

Geography

Qatar, a small peninsula country in the Persian Gulf, is surrounded by Bahrain, Saudi Arabia, and the United Arab Emirates. It has a population of roughly 2.6 million people and occupies a total area of 11,586 square kilometers. Despite its small size and advantageous location, Qatar has emerged as a significant player in the international scene, both economically and politically.

Qatar is well-known for its beautiful geography and diverse landscapes. The country is mainly composed of a flat desert, with a few oasis-like areas along its eastern coast. The country's highest point is Qurayn Abu al Bawl, which stands at 103 meters above sea level. In the north, the Al Shamal coast features long stretches of beach, while the south is known for its mangrove forests and wetlands.

Qatar is home to a diverse diversity of wildlife, including various species of migratory birds who make the nation their home during the winter months. The nation is also home to numerous rare species of reptiles and animals, including the Arabian Oryx and the Arabian Desert Fox.

The climate of the nation is mainly hot and dry, with temperatures ranging from 28°C in winter to 40°C in summer. Rainfall is very rare in Qatar, with an average of only 3-4 inches per year.

Qatar's economy is mostly dependent on its oil and natural gas reserves. The country is also a major exporter of petrochemicals and aluminum and has invested heavily in its infrastructure in recent years. Additionally, it serves as a hub for global corporations and institutions like the United Nations.

Doha, which is found on the nation's eastern coast, serves as Qatar's capital. Doha is a thriving city with a plethora of contemporary buildings, cultural attractions, and luxury hotels. Education City, a center for foreign institutions and research organizations, is also located in the city.

Qatar is an intriguing country, full of natural beauty and economic potential. Its strategic location and wealth of resources make it an important player in the global arena, and its diverse landscapes, vibrant cities, and unusual animals make it a popular destination for visitors and explorers alike.

CHAPTER TWO

Planning Your Trip

Budgeting

Budgeting is an essential component of planning a successful trip to Qatar. Developing a budget helps travelers ensure they have enough money to cover their expenses while traveling. Before embarking on a trip to Qatar, travelers should consider the cost of transportation, accommodation, food, and entertainment. By creating a budget, travelers can ensure they can enjoy their trip without worrying about a lack of funds.

The cost of transportation is a major factor to consider when planning a trip to Qatar. Qatar is serviced by large international airports, including Hamad International Airport in Doha, and passengers may opt to fly into the country or take a bus or train. Depending on the destination, the cost of transportation can vary significantly. For instance, a flight from New York to Doha could cost several hundred dollars, while a bus from Dubai to Doha may cost just a few dozen dollars. Moreover, traveling inside Qatar might be pricey. Taxis and rental cars are widely available, but travelers may find that taking public transportation, such as the national bus service, is more cost-effective.

Accommodation is another major expense to consider when budgeting for a trip to Qatar. Hotels are widely available in Qatar and range from luxury five-star establishments to budget-friendly options. Prices can vary significantly depending on location and amenities. For instance, a hotel in downtown Doha will likely be more expensive than a hotel on the outskirts of the city. Additionally, travelers may choose to stay in an Airbnb or comparable rental property. This option can be more affordable than a hotel and can also provide a more authentic experience.

Food is another important factor to consider when budgeting for a trip to Qatar. Qatar has a wide variety of cuisine, from traditional Arabic dishes to international flavors. Eating out can be costly, so travelers may want to consider purchasing groceries to prepare their own meals. Additionally, Qatar has a number of street food stands and markets where travelers can purchase inexpensive meals.

Finally, travelers should factor in entertainment costs when budgeting for a trip to Qatar. Qatar is home to a number of cultural attractions, from museums to monuments. Additionally, travelers can take advantage of the country's stunning beaches, or take a day trip to explore the desert. Of course, Qatar also offers a wide range of shopping opportunities and nightlife options. There are numerous activities to choose from, but before committing to one, travelers should consider the cost of admission or any additional fees.

Budgeting is an essential part of planning a successful trip to Qatar. Travelers should consider the cost of transportation, accommodation, food, and entertainment when creating a budget. By doing so, they can ensure they have enough funds to enjoy their trip without worrying about a lack of money.

When To Visit

Qatar is a small but fascinating country situated in the Middle East. It is home to a diverse range of cultures, with a vibrant history and a booming economy. With its stunning landscapes, world-class attractions, and unique heritage, Qatar is an ideal destination for travelers looking to explore the region.

When planning a trip to Qatar, it is important to consider the best time to visit. Qatar's climate is hot and dry throughout the year, with temperatures ranging from 24°C in the winter months to 40°C in the summer. The best time to visit Qatar is between November and April when temperatures are cooler and rainfall is minimal.

During this time, Qatar's attractions are in full bloom, and visitors can experience a range of cultural activities and events. The country also hosts several international festivals and exhibitions throughout the winter, including the Doha International Film Festival and the Qatar International Food Festival.

It is also important to note that Qatar observes Ramadan, the Islamic month of fasting, from May to June. Although the country's attractions remain open during this period, visitors should be aware that alcohol is not served in restaurants and cafes during Ramadan.

In addition to the weather and festivals, it is also important to consider the cost of visiting Qatar when planning a trip. Qatar is a relatively expensive destination, with accommodation and transportation costs being higher than in other parts of the region. Prices vary depending on the season and demand, so it is best to research the cost of flights and hotels before visiting.

The best time to visit Qatar is between November and April when temperatures are cooler and there are fewer crowds. During this period, visitors can enjoy a range of cultural activities and events, and take advantage of the country's attractions. However, travelers should also consider the cost of their visit and be aware of Ramadan when planning their trip.

How To Get There

Although arranging a trip to Qatar may be tough, with the right preparation and help, it can also be enjoyable and rewarding. Qatar is a small but diverse Middle Eastern country with a rich cultural and historical heritage and a wide range of activities. To ensure a successful vacation, all preparation-related variables, such as hotel, sightseeing, and budgeting, must be considered.

The first stage in vacation planning is to choose a mode of transportation. Traveling directly to Qatar from the United States or Canada is available with Qatar Airlines, which has the shortest flight route. Those going from different parts of the world may need to take several flights. Going by land or sea is another alternative, although it may be a longer and more expensive adventure.

The next step is to decide on an accommodation. There are several hotels and resorts in Qatar from which to pick, so it is essential to evaluate them all and choose one that meets the traveler's needs and preferences. Financial consideration and ensuring that the hotel meets the budget criteria are also important.

After you've decided on a mode of transportation and a place to stay, plan your sightseeing. Qatar has both modern attractions, such as the well-known Qatar National Museum, and historic cities and monuments. Other activities like sandboarding, camel riding, dune buggy, and others are also offered. To make the most of your stay in Qatar, you must plan ahead of time and research the numerous activities.

Finally, making a budget is an important component of planning a trip. It is important to consider the cost of transport, hotel, and sightseeing, as well as the cost of meals and other expenses. The cost of any prospective visas or licenses must also be considered. Following through on the agreed-upon budget will assist to make the vacation successful and enjoyable.

A holiday to Qatar requires a thorough consideration of all important variables. Visitors may ensure that their vacation to Qatar is successful and enjoyable by researching their options for hotel, food, and sightseeing, as well as creating and keeping to a budget.

Traveling Documents

It is important to plan and prepare for a trip to Qatar, which includes getting the legal papers necessary for admittance. When crossing international borders, travelers must check that their paperwork is up to date and in excellent shape. A valid passport and visa are required. Passengers may need supplementary documents such as health certificates, travel insurance, and other paperwork depending on their intended purpose and length of stay.

A passport is a formal document issued by a government to indicate that a person is a citizen of that country. It is necessary for international travel into, out of, and within other countries. All travelers to Qatar must have a valid passport with at least six months remaining before it expires. In addition to a passport, a visa is necessary for admission into Qatar, and the kind of visa required varies depending on the purpose of the visit. Travelers visiting Qatar for business or pleasure, for example, will need a tourist visa, whilst those visiting for a job, education, or medical treatment would require a different kind of visa.

Tourists may be required to get additional paperwork in order to enter Qatar. Visitors from certain countries, for example, may be required to provide a recent health certificate issued by a physician recognized by the Qatari government. Visitors who want to stay in Qatar for more than 30 days must get a residence permit, and those who intend to stay for more than 90 days must obtain an entry permit.

Travelers may consider purchasing travel insurance before traveling. This kind of insurance may cover medical fees as well as other costs incurred as a consequence of unanticipated events such as accidents, illness, and other emergencies. Travelers should carefully research their insurance options since some policies may exclude particular activities or locations.

Visitors to Qatar must ensure that they have the necessary documentation to enter the country. A valid passport and visa are necessary, and depending on the length of stay, other documents such as health records, travel insurance, and residence permits may be required. To avoid problems upon arrival, it is important to plan ahead of time and grasp the exact conditions for entry into Qatar.

Local Costumes and Etiquette of the people

Qatar is a country with a vibrant culture steeped in regional customs and etiquette. Qataris take pride in their culture and demonstrate it in their daily lives, from the elaborate hospitality rituals to the traditional clothing worn by the people.

The traditional dress worn by Qataris separates them from other civilizations. The typical costume is a thawb, a long, loose-fitting white shirt worn by males with a bisht, a long, embroidered cloak. Women often cover their hair with a hijab and wear long, black robes known as abayas. Both men and women wear gahfiya, a circle hat, and keffiyeh, a headpiece worn as a statement of pride in one's ancestry.

Qatari hospitality norms are based on the concepts of respect and compassion. "Assalamu alaikum" is a polite method of greeting someone (peace be upon you). A hug or handshake is typically exchanged following this phrase, depending on the two people's relationship. Traditionally, visitors are offered cups of Arabic coffee and dates, or qahwa and khajur, as a sign of welcome.

To maintain respect and decency at the dinner table, particular etiquette requirements must be followed. It is important to wait until everyone has gotten their meal before eating. Additionally, before commencing, one must wait for the eldest diner at the table to begin eating. It is also considered disrespectful to leave the table before everyone has finished.

Moreover, Qataris follow a number of societal customs. Elders must always be respected, and humility must always be shown. Confrontations and arguments should also be avoided since they are considered impolite.

Qatar's vibrant culture is reflected in the local clothes and manners of the populace. Qataris take pride in their culture and demonstrate it in their daily lives, from the elaborate hospitality rituals to the traditional clothing worn by the people. Respect and humility are highly valued in Qatari culture, and these ideals are reflected in the different customs and etiquette that the people adhere to.

Languages spoken in the country

Qatar is a small yet diverse Arab country in the Middle East. Its population is largely made up of people of many races, and a wide range of languages are spoken there. English, Hindi, Urdu, Tagalog, Persian, and Chinese are among the many languages spoken in Qatar, in addition to Arabic, the country's official language.

The official language of Qatar is Arabic, which is spoken by the vast majority of the people. It is the official language of Qatar, as well as the language of business, education, and the majority of the people. Both radio and television use Arabic as their major language. It is also the language used in religious rituals and rites.

English is widely spoken in Qatar, and it is the primary language for media, education, and business. English, in addition to being the language of official documents, is also the language of worldwide communication. In addition, several colleges and universities teach in English.

Several people in Qatar, particularly in the Indian and Pakistani communities, speak Hindi and Urdu. These languages are used in both education and the media, such as radio and television.

Tagalog is used by the Filipino population in Qatar for communication, as well as on radio and television. Tagalog is also widely used in schools and is the chosen language of many Filipino-owned businesses.

Qatar also boasts a sizable Chinese and Iranian community. The Iranian people speak Persian, which is also used in media such as radio and television. Mandarin is used in media and education, and the Chinese people speak it.

Qatar is a multilingual country with many distinct languages spoken. The official language of Qatar is Arabic, which is spoken by the vast majority of the people. Together with Arabic, English, Hindi, Urdu, Tagalog, Persian, and Mandarin are commonly spoken in Qatar. All of these languages contribute to Qatar's cultural variety, and they are used in the media, schools, and businesses.

Phrases For Travel

Qatar is a lovely and adventurous Middle Eastern country. Qatar has something for everyone, from its vast deserts to its vibrant cities. With the country's distinct and diverse culture, knowing the proper things to say when vacationing in Qatar is critical. Making friends, understanding the culture, and finding your way around may all be made simpler with the right terminology. We'll look at some crucial terms and idioms for traveling in Qatar here.

One of the most important terms to learn is Marhaba, a greeting used in Qatar. It is a show of respect, similar to saying "hello" in English. Since it is nice and respectful, this greeting should always be given when meeting someone when traveling in Qatar.

You should also learn "shukran," the Arabic term for "thank you," which is also used to convey gratitude and appreciation. Since you will come across these terms and phrases often when traveling in Qatar, it is crucial to know how to communicate with them.

It is also important to learn some basic food-related language. While visiting Qatar, you will most likely come across a variety of wonderful delicacies such as shawarma, falafel, and kabab. It may be useful to know some basic food-related terminology while ordering at restaurants or when grocery shopping. For example, "halal" refers to food that Muslims are permitted to eat, but "sujuk" refers to a specific kind of sausage. By being aware of these idioms, you may guarantee that you order the correct kind of food.

Finally, there are certain terms and phrases related to directions and transportation that are useful while traveling in Qatar. Knowing how to ask for directions and how to hail a taxi may be essential when traveling across the country. To request directions, use "Ana la'aalt," which translates as "I desire to go." Similarly, "mawjuud?" may be used to enquire if a site is nearby and indicates "is there?" Knowing these terms can help you travel to Qatar.

Traveling in Qatar may be exciting and rewarding. To ensure the success of your trip, you must be able to communicate in the appropriate language. You will be able to adjust to the culture and move about more quickly if you learn a few basic greetings, culinary, and navigational words. With a little preparation and research, you can make the most of your trip to Qatar.

CHAPTER THREE

Transportation

Major Cities In The Country

Qatar is a small yet developed country in the Middle East. It is a highly diversified country with major cities, each having something unique to offer both people and visitors. From the contemporary metropolis of Doha to the old city of Al Khor, Qatar offers something for everyone. In this guide, we'll look at Qatar's major cities and see what makes them special.

The majority of Qataris live in Doha, the country's capital and largest city. There are several cultural monuments there, including museums, art galleries, and historical places.

The city is an important regional center for trade and finance, with a thriving commercial sector. Doha is also known for its active nightlife, which includes a wide range of restaurants, bars, and nightclubs.

Al Khor, Qatar's second-largest city, is located on the country's northern coast. It is a historical city with roots dating back to the fifteenth century. Numerous archeological structures and cultural landmarks, including as fortresses, mosques, and museums, may still be seen in Al Khor today. It is also well-known among tourists for having gorgeous beaches where you can go fishing or snorkeling.

Al Wakra is a small village located on Qatar's southeast coast. It is well-known for its stunning beaches, lively markets, and traditional architecture. Al Wakra is a popular spot for travelers to rest and relax since it is also home to a number of eateries, taverns, and cafés.

Al Rayyan, located just west of Doha, is Qatar's fourth-largest city. There are a variety of cultural institutions, shopping malls, amusement parks, and other activities there. Al Rayyan also houses the Qatar National Museum, which has a collection of historic treasures from throughout the country.

Qatar has major cities, each of which offers something unique to offer both people and visitors. From the bustling capital city of Doha to the historic city of Al Khor, Qatar offers something for everyone. Qatar has something for everyone, whether they are looking for culture, adventure, or leisure.

Conveyance

The small but strong Arabian Gulf country of Qatar is known for its cutting-edge infrastructure, cutting-edge transportation systems, and first-rate services. Despite its modest size, Qatar boasts a well-developed and efficient transportation infrastructure that provides a number of options for both local and international travelers. In this guide, we will look at Qatar's transportation system and its many components.

The three primary divisions of Qatar's transportation system are public transportation, private transportation, and air travel. Buses, taxis, and trains are the three primary types of public transit in Qatar. Buses are preferred over other modes of transportation by locals because they are handy and fairly priced. In Qatar, a huge bus network connects major cities, towns, and villages. Taxis are widely available and widely used in most major cities. Qatar also has an advanced and efficient rail system, with lines connecting the nation's capital, Doha, to nearby cities.

Automobiles and car rental services are the most common modes of private transportation in Qatar. Cars are the most popular mode of transportation in Qatar because they give the comfort and convenience of private transportation. There are also private rental companies that provide both long-term and short-term car, van, and truck rentals.

Air travel is the third most common means of transportation in Qatar. Qatar Airlines, the country's official airline, provides both domestic and international services to major cities throughout the world. Qatar has many international airports, including Hamad International Airport and Doha International Airport.

Qatar's wide road network includes motorways, expressways, arterial highways, and local roads. The highway system connects the country's biggest cities and towns, making it the fastest and most efficient form of transit. While arterial roads connect major cities, expressways are shorter routes that connect towns and villages. Local highways give access to residential areas and villages.

Qatar has a strong maritime transportation system in addition to a fantastic road network. Qatar has many ports, including the Doha Port and the Ruwais Port. Ferries go from these ports to Bahrain, the United Arab Emirates, and other Gulf countries. Moreover, Qatar has a variety of smaller ports that are used for fishing as well as recreational purposes.

Because of Qatar's wide and efficient transit infrastructure, both local and international visitors may pick from a variety of transportation options. Qatar is well-equipped to meet the needs of travelers from all over the world, thanks to its extensive road network, modern airports, and efficient maritime transportation systems.

Airports

Qatar is a Middle Eastern country located in the Persian Gulf. Qatar, which has a population of 2.77 million people, has airports that all provide international services. In addition to functioning as a vital hub for international travel, these airports provide a variety of services and amenities to travelers. In this guide, we'll look at Qatar's major airports and discuss the services they provide.

Hamad International Airport is Qatar's primary international airport (DOH). It is situated in Doha, the country of Qatar's capital. Hamad International Airport, one of the world's newest airports, features a range of amenities and services, including an elegant lounge, food choices, duty-free shopping, and much more. This airport is one of the busiest in the world, with over 35 million passengers passing through each year.

The US Air Force is the primary user of Al Udeid Air Base (XJD), which is located in Qatar's desert. This military aviation complex has two runways, a passenger terminal, and several other amenities. It can also convey a large amount of cargo, making it an important hub for military actions in the region.

The city of Al Mazrouah is home to Al Mazrouah International Airport (XUZ), a major hub for Qatar Airlines. This airport serves many international cities, including those in Europe, Asia, and the Middle East. At Al Mazrouah International Airport, modern conveniences such as self-check-in kiosks are accessible, as well as a range of services such as a VIP lounge, duty-free shopping, and a selection of restaurants.

Al Khor International Airport (AKH) is located in the city of Al Khor and serves as a major hub for Qatar Airlines. This airport offers a variety of services and facilities, such as a VIP lounge, duty-free shopping, food choices, and other businesses. Al Khor International Airport, an important hub for international travel, can also handle large amounts of freight.

Al-Ruwais Airport (XRW), located in the city of Al Ruwais, serves as a major hub for Qatar Airlines. This airport offers a variety of services and amenities, including a VIP lounge, duty-free shopping, food choices, and several other attractions. Since it can handle large amounts of freight, this airport acts as an important hub for international traffic.

The US Air Force is the primary user of Al Udeid Air Base (XJD), which is located in Qatar's desert. This military aviation complex has two runways, a passenger terminal, and several other amenities. It can also convey a large amount of cargo, making it an important hub for military actions in the region.

Al-Barka Airport (XBK) is a major hub for Qatar Airlines, located in the city of Al Barka. This airport offers a variety of services and amenities, including a VIP lounge, duty-free shopping, food choices, and several other attractions. Al-Barka Airport is an important hub for international travel since it can handle large amounts of cargo.

Qatar's airports all provide international service. In addition to functioning as a vital hub for international travel, these airports provide a variety of services and amenities to travelers. Hamad International Airport serves as Qatar's primary international airport, while the US Air Force mostly utilizes Al Udeid Air Base and Al-Barka Airport. Qatar Airlines has major hubs at Al Mazrouah International Airport, Al Khor International Airport, Al-Ruwais Airport, and Al-Barka Airport. These airports are ideal for foreign visitors since they each provide cutting-edge services and technology.

Taxi

Qatar, a Middle Eastern Arab country, is well-known for its lofty towers, beautiful beaches, and luxury hotels. Being a growing nation, the number of people using taxi services to go has greatly expanded. Travelers in Qatar may choose between many taxi charge types based on their needs. People who wish to travel throughout the country should be informed of the different price categories.

In Qatar, the "regular" fare is the first category of taxi charges. This ticket is the cheapest option and is suitable for short trips, such as those from a hotel to a nearby restaurant or activity. It is decided by the distance traveled and is often suitable. The regular fare is also the most often used kind of fare in Qatar.

The second kind of taxi price is the "fixed rate." Although somewhat more expensive than a conventional ticket, this tariff provides a set amount that consumers must pay regardless of the distance traveled. This is a good option for individuals looking for a more consistent supper or who are on a long journey.

The third kind of fare is the "shared" fare. This charge is frequently paid by those who wish to divide the cost of a taxi ride with other clients. Since the charge is based on the number of persons in the cab, if there are two passengers, they will each pay half of the cost. Those looking to save expenditures may find this to be an excellent option.

The fourth kind of fee is the "per hour" price. This fare is best suited for passengers who need to make many stops or who have long itineraries. The charge for persons who need to take their time and are unfamiliar with the area is decided by the length of the travel.

The "airport" fare is the sixth fare type. While somewhat more expensive than the normal ticket, this fee also includes a set payment for airport transfers. This might be a good option for people looking for a more consistent fare or who are unfamiliar with the area.

The "special" fare is the sixth fare type. This dinner is often provided on important occasions such as birthdays, weddings, and anniversaries. The cost is sometimes more than the normal menu, but it might be an excellent way to commemorate a special event.

The "night" fare is the seventh and final fare category. This fee is often used for late-night trips and is more than the usual ticket. The expense of nighttime travel is often greater due to the added hazard.

Anybody considering a trip to Qatar should be aware of the different taxi fare categories. While deciding on a mode of transportation, it is important to consider all of your options since each kind of ticket has pros and drawbacks of its own. Knowing the different rates allows passengers to choose the kind of fare that is most suited to their needs.

Car Rentals

Although being a small Middle Eastern country, Qatar boasts an impressive infrastructure, particularly when it comes to car rental services. The huge number of providers and prices available makes it easy to get a car rental in Qatar that meets your requirements. The top automobile rental firms in Qatar are listed below.

It is hardly surprising that Hertz, one of the world's most well-known car rental companies, has a presence in Qatar. Hertz provides both high-end and low-cost cars. Customers who make online bookings get savings and have access to customer service representatives 24 hours a day, seven days a week. Hertz also offers airport pickup and drop-off services.

Thrifty is another well-known car rental business in Qatar. Thrifty offers a wide range of autos, from high-end models to more inexpensive variants. They also provide discounts on drop-off services, airport transfers, and internet bookings. Thrifty has a customer support team that is accessible around the clock in addition to a choice of supplemental services like vehicle insurance and roadside assistance.

Sixt is another fantastic option for hiring a car in Qatar. This company is well-known for providing high-quality vehicles at reasonable prices. They provide a wide range of vehicles, from high-end to low-cost models. They also provide discounts on drop-off services, airport transfers, and internet bookings. Sixt also provides motor insurance, roadside assistance, and a customer service team that is accessible 24 hours a day, seven days a week.

Enterprise is another well-known rental car company in Qatar. This company is well-known for providing excellent customer service and a wide range of autos, from high-end models to more inexpensive choices. They also provide discounts on drop-off services, airport transfers, and internet bookings. Enterprise provides roadside assistance, motor insurance, and customer service.

Avis is another fantastic rental car business in Qatar. This company is well-known for producing high-quality vehicles at reasonable prices. They provide a wide range of vehicles, from high-end to low-cost models. They also provide discounts on drop-off services, airport transfers, and internet bookings. Avis provides roadside assistance, motor insurance, and customer service.

Europcar is another well-known vehicle rental business in Qatar. This firm is internationally famous for its high-standard vehicles and great customer service. They provide a wide range of vehicles, from high-end to low-cost models. They also provide discounts on drop-off services, airport transfers, and internet bookings. Moreover, Europcar provides motor insurance, roadside assistance, and 24-hour customer service personnel.

Budget is Qatar's last notable car rental firm. This company is well-known for providing high-quality vehicles at reasonable prices. They provide a wide range of vehicles, from high-end to low-cost models. They also provide discounts on drop-off services, airport transfers, and internet bookings. Budget also provides motor insurance, roadside assistance, and a customer service team that is accessible around the clock.

There is no shortage of vehicle rental companies in Qatar. Each of the aforementioned vendors offers high-quality autos at reasonable prices, as well as a range of additional services. Choosing the car rental company that best matches your needs necessitates research since each has pros and cons of its own.

Train Stations

Qatar, a small but important Middle Eastern country, functions as a regional transportation hub. There are seven railway stations there, and both inhabitants and visitors use them. These stations provide a variety of services, such as access to local bus routes and intercity and regional train connections. In this guide, we'll go over each of Qatar's key train stations in further depth, as well as the services they provide.

The first railway station on the list is Al Wakra Station, which is located in the city of Al Wakra. This station is served by both the Qatar Railway Company (QRC) and the Qatar Public Transport Company (QPTC). It provides access to other regional communities like Al Khor and Al Jeryan, as well as interstate services to and from Doha. Many bus routes begin at Al Wakra Station.

The second railway station is Al Wukair Station, which is located in the city of Al

Wukair. At this station, the QRC and QPTC both run intercity services to and from Doha. Al Wukair Station also acts as the starting point for several local bus routes.

The third railway station is Al Khor Station, which is located in the city of Al Khor. At this station, the QRC provides intercity services to and from Doha. In addition, Al Khor Station is the beginning point for a variety of local bus routes.

The fourth railway station is Al Jeryan Station, which is located in the city of Al Jeryan. This station is operated by the QRC and provides connections to different regional cities as well as interstate services to and from Doha. Al Jeryan Station serves as the starting point for a variety of regional bus routes.

The sixth railway station is Al Rayyan Station, which is located in the city of Al Rayyan. This station is operated by the QRC and provides connections to different regional cities as well as interstate services to and from Doha. Moreover, Al Rayyan Station acts as the beginning point for many bus lines.

The sixth railway station is Al Kharaij Station, which is located in the city of Al Kharaij. This station is operated by the QRC and provides connections to different regional cities as well as interstate services to and from Doha. In addition, Al Kharaij Station is the beginning point for a variety of local bus routes.

Al Wakrah Station, located in the city of Al Wakrah, is the eighth railway station in the country. This station is operated by the QRC and provides connections to different regional cities as well as interstate services to and from Doha. In addition, Al Wakrah Station is the beginning point for a variety of local bus routes.

In Qatar, there are seven unique railway stations served by both the Qatar Railway Company and the Qatar Public Transport Company. These stations connect to a variety of regional cities as well as interstate services to and from Doha. Each of these stations is also the starting point for many local bus routes. As a consequence, the most important railway stations in Qatar offer a vital and efficient mode of transit for both inhabitants and visitors.

CHAPTER FOUR

Accommodations

Hotels

Qatar, a small but fast-rising Middle Eastern country, has earned a reputation as a sanctuary for luxury and elegance. Because of its beautiful beaches, amazing architecture, and booming economy, Qatar is swiftly moving to the top of the world's tourist attractions list. Qatar has some of the best locations to stay in the world, with an ever-expanding collection of luxury hotels. The top hotels in Qatar are listed below.

1. The St. Regis Doha is an opulent hotel with stunning views of the Persian Gulf and the

city. It is located in the geographic center of Doha. The hotel features an excellent spa, an outdoor pool, and many eating choices. The guest rooms are spacious, attractively decorated, and outfitted with first-rate amenities.

2. The Ritz-Carlton Doha is a luxurious hotel located near the Corniche in Doha, Qatar. The hotel offers stunning views of the city and the Gulf. The hotel has a variety of culinary choices, a luxurious spa, and a fitness center. The marble bathrooms in the guest suites are spacious and opulent.

3. The Four Seasons Hotel Doha is a five-star hotel in the heart of the city. The hotel offers first-rate amenities in addition to a lovely outdoor pool, a full-service spa, and a variety of restaurants and bars. The guest rooms are

spacious, attractively decorated, and outfitted with first-rate amenities.

4. The Sheraton Doha Hotel and Resort is lovely in Qatar on the Corniche. The hotel offers stunning views of the city and the Gulf. The hotel has a variety of culinary choices, a luxurious spa, and a fitness center. The marble bathrooms in the guest suites are spacious and opulent.

5. The W Doha Hotel and Residences is a five-star hotel located in the heart of Doha. The hotel has a variety of culinary choices, a luxurious spa, and a fitness center. The guest rooms are spacious, attractively decorated, and outfitted with first-rate amenities.

6. The InterContinental Doha is a luxurious hotel located in the heart of Doha. The hotel

has a variety of culinary choices, a luxurious spa, and a fitness center. The marble bathrooms in the guest suites are spacious and opulent.

7. The Ritz-Carlton Hotel and Residences Doha is a five-star hotel located near the Corniche. The hotel offers first-rate amenities in addition to a lovely outdoor pool, a full-service spa, and a variety of restaurants and bars. The guest rooms are spacious, attractively decorated, and outfitted with first-rate amenities.

8. The Marsa Malaz Kempinski The Pearl is an elegant hotel on Qatar's coast. The hotel offers stunning views of the city and the Gulf. The hotel has a variety of culinary choices, a luxurious spa, and a fitness center. The

marble bathrooms in the guest suites are spacious and opulent.

9. The Oryx Rotana is a five-star hotel located in the heart of Doha. The hotel has a variety of culinary choices, a luxurious spa, and a fitness center. The guest rooms are spacious, attractively decorated, and outfitted with first-rate amenities.

10. The Sharq Village and Spa is a wonderful hotel located on Qatar's coastline. The hotel offers stunning views of the city and the Gulf. The hotel has a variety of culinary choices, a luxurious spa, and a fitness center. The marble bathrooms in the guest suites are spacious and opulent.

Qatar is proven to be one of the world's top destinations for luxury and extravagance, with its numerous hotels. The Sharq Village and Spa and the St. Regis Doha are two of the world's best hotels. Whether you're looking for a luxurious vacation or a place to stay with stunning views of the city and the Gulf, Qatar has plenty of options.

Resorts

Qatar is a fast-rising tourist destination with a diverse selection of sights and activities. With its beautiful beaches, cutting-edge architecture, and interesting culture, Qatar attracts travelers from all over the world. But, with the multitude of possibilities, choosing which resort to stay at may be difficult. Here is a list of the greatest resorts in Qatar to help you make the best decision.

The W Doha Hotel & Residences is at the top of the list. The W Doha has luxury amenities such as a spa, a private beach, and a rooftop infinity pool. It is located in the vibrant West Bay neighborhood. Guests may also dine in the on-site restaurant, which serves a variety of international cuisine.

The following is the Al Messila Resort & Spa, which is situated on the outskirts of the desert. This resort offers a variety of activities, including camel rides, yoga sessions, and equestrian riding. Guests may also enjoy the resort's exclusive spa treatments, which use traditional Arabic techniques.

The third hotel on the list is Banana Island Resort Doha. Kayaking, snorkeling, and paddle boarding are just a few of the sports accessible at this private island resort. There is also an on-site movie theater and a variety of cuisines accessible to visitors.

The Sharq Village & Spa, located in the heart of Doha, is ranked fourth. This resort's features include an outdoor pool, spa, and fitness center, to name a few. Visitors may experience a variety of diverse cuisines in addition to typical Qatari dishes.

The Marsa Malaz Kempinski, located on Pearl-Qatar Island, is ranked sixth. This resort has various amenities, including a spa, a private beach, and an outdoor pool. Visitors may try meals from all around the globe in addition to traditional Qatari dishes.

The Kempinski Residences & Suites, located in the heart of Doha, is ranked sixth. This resort's features include an outdoor pool, spa, and fitness center, to name a few. Visitors may experience a variety of diverse cuisines in addition to typical Qatari dishes.

The Ritz-Carlton Doha, located in the heart of Qatar, is ranked seventh. This resort's features include an outdoor pool, spa, and fitness center, to name a few. Visitors may experience a variety of diverse cuisines in addition to typical Qatari dishes.

The Four Seasons Hotel Doha, located in the heart of the city, is placed seventh. This resort's features include an outdoor pool, spa, and fitness center, to name a few. Visitors may experience a variety of diverse cuisines in addition to typical Qatari dishes.

The Grand Hyatt Doha, located in the heart of Qatar, ranks ninth. This resort's features include an outdoor pool, spa, and fitness center, to name a few. Visitors may experience a variety of diverse cuisines in addition to typical Qatari dishes.

The Sheraton Grand Doha, a prominently located hotel, ranks tenth. This resort's features include an outdoor pool, spa, and fitness center, to name a few. Visitors may experience a variety of diverse cuisines in addition to typical Qatari dishes.

The best resorts in Qatar provide a wide range of services and recreational options to their customers. From luxury spas and private beaches to genuine Qatari cuisine, these resorts offer everything you need for the perfect getaway. Any of these resorts will ensure you have the best vacation possible, whether you're looking for a unique experience or a luxurious refuge.

Camping Sites

Although Qatar is a small country on the Arabian Peninsula, it features some of the most beautiful camping areas in the region. Qatar offers a broad choice of options for outdoor lovers looking for a good camping experience, from spectacular desert vistas to beautiful beaches. Regardless of your degree of expertise in camping or being outside, there are several ways to explore Qatar's wonderful outdoors.

The following are the best camping spots in Qatar:

1. Al Thakhira Beach Camp: Located on Qatar's eastern coast, Al Thakhira Beach Camp is a perfect place for enjoying the Arabian Sea. Our beach camp is set on a distant beach, giving a peaceful and relaxing atmosphere. The camp offers a variety of activities as well as basic amenities such as bathrooms and showers. There is something for everyone at Al Thakhira Beach Camp, including kayaking, swimming, snorkeling, boat rides, and fishing.

2. The Khor Al Udaid Beach Camp on Qatar's western shore provides views of the Arabian Gulf. It offers a one-of-a-kind camping experience with its magnificent beaches, gorgeous coral reefs, and diverse wildlife. Swimming, snorkeling, fishing, and kayaking are just a few of the activities available. In

addition, the camp offers basics such as bathrooms and showers.

3. Al Khor Beach Camp: This beach camp is situated on Qatar's eastern coast in the Al Khor area. It offers a variety of leisure possibilities and amenities, such as bathrooms and showers. Jet skiing and fishing are only two of the activities available on the magnificent seashore. The gorgeous beaches, crystal-clear streams, and diverse wildlife of the camp all contribute to a memorable camping experience.

4. Al Khor Inland Camp: Located in the Al Khor area, this inland camp is great for wildlife aficionados. Our camp is situated in a beautiful desert oasis, near a broad range of wildlife. You can keep yourself entertained by doing activities like bird watching, hiking,

and camping. The camp offers a variety of activities as well as basic amenities such as bathrooms and showers.

5. Al Wakrah Beach Camp is situated on a lonely beach in the Al Wakrah district. There are numerous things to do there, and the atmosphere is tranquil. There are activities for everyone at the beach camp, such as kayaking, fishing, and swimming.

6. Al Wakrah Inland Camp: This inland camp in the Al Wakrah area offers a unique camping experience. In a desert oasis, it is surrounded by gorgeous flora and a diverse range of species. You can keep yourself entertained by doing activities like bird watching, hiking, and camping. In addition, the camp offers basics such as bathrooms and showers.

7. Al Zubara Beach Camp: Al Zubara Beach Camp is situated on Qatar's western coast, overlooking the Arabian Gulf. It offers a one-of-a-kind camping experience with its stunning beaches, crystal-clear oceans, and diverse wildlife. Swimming, snorkeling, fishing, and kayaking are just a few of the activities available. In addition, the camp offers basics such as bathrooms and showers.

8. Al Jumaili Beach Camp is a distant beach camp in the Al Khor area. There are numerous things to do there, and the atmosphere is tranquil. There are activities for everyone at the beach camp, such as kayaking, fishing, and swimming.

9. Al Wakrah Desert Camp: This desert camp in the Al Wakrah area offers a unique camping experience. It is surrounded by a

large amount of sand and dunes, creating a tranquil and pleasant setting. The camp offers a variety of activities as well as basic amenities such as bathrooms and showers. Camel rides and sandboarding are among the activities available at the desert camp.

10. Al Khor Desert Camp: This desert camp in the Al Khor area offers a unique camping experience. It is surrounded by a large amount of sand and dunes, creating a tranquil and pleasant setting. The camp offers a variety of activities as well as basic amenities such as bathrooms and showers. Camel rides and sandboarding are among the activities available at the desert camp.

In Qatar, there are several camping locations, each with its own unique set of amenities. Whether you're looking for a distant beach camp or a desert hideaway, Qatar offers something for everyone. Qatar is a fantastic destination for outdoor enthusiasts due to its magnificent scenery, abundant wildlife, and diverse choice of activities.

CHAPTER FIVE

Sightseeing

Ancient Monuments

Qatar has a number of historic sites and monuments, some of which date back more than two thousand years. These sites are a must-see for anybody visiting Qatar since they give a unique glimpse into the country's rich history and culture. This book will explore the most important ancient buildings in Qatar, as well as their historical significance.

The Al Zubarah Fort, completed in 1938, is one of Qatar's most iconic structures. This fort, located near Al Zubarah, serves as a memorial to the nation's famous maritime legacy. It was originally established as a base for merchants and pearl divers to protect their merchandise from pirates. Visitors to the fort, which is now a UNESCO World Heritage Site, may visit the grounds and learn more about Qatar's history.

The Barzan Towers are yet another important historical landmark in Qatar. These two towers, located near the capital Doha, were erected in the late 1800s and acted as watchtowers. The towers are now a famous tourist site, with visitors able to enjoy a breathtaking view of the city from the top.

Another popular historical landmark in Qatar is the Souq Waqif. Its vibrant marketplace stems from the 16th century and is one of the Middle East's oldest traditional markets. Visitors may explore the market's meandering pathways and shop for anything from spices and incense to traditional clothing and jewelry.

The Doha Corniche is a historic building that has been transformed into a modern public space. This four-kilometer beachside walkway along Doha Bay provides stunning views of the city skyline. Visitors may walk along the Corniche and enjoy the various cafes, cafés, and parks that they pass.

These are just the best of Qatar's historic buildings. Each of these places has a unique history that provides travelers with a glimpse into Qatar's past. Stop by these sites, which vary from the Al Zubarah Fort to the Doha Corniche, if you want to discover more about Qatar's rich history and culture.

Museums

Qatar is home to some of the world's most spectacular and unusual museums. For locals and visitors alike, the country offers a multitude of historical and cultural sites, such as the Sheikh Faisal Bin Qassim Al Thani Museum and the Museum of Islamic Art. The top museums in Qatar are listed in the list below.

The Museum of Islamic Art, located in the heart of Doha, has a diverse collection of Islamic art from throughout the world. Among other different media, the museum's holdings include calligraphy, textiles, and even carpets. Apart from its great permanent collection, the museum often hosts a variety of temporary exhibitions.

The Sheikh Faisal Bin Qassim Al Thani Museum is located to the north of Doha, near Al Khor. The museum has over 15,000 antiquities, which range from traditional weapons and jewelry to historical documents and photographs. It is dedicated to Sheikh Faisal, one of Qatar's most renowned people, and celebrates his legacy.

The Arab Museum of Modern Art, located in the heart of Doha, is the region's first museum entirely dedicated to modern art. The museum's collection includes works by some of the most well-known Arab and international artists, including Youssef Nabil and Hassan Sharif. During the year, the museum also hosts a slew of one-of-a-kind exhibitions and events.

The National Museum of Qatar, located in the country's capital, is one of the most substantial museums in the Middle East. The museum's collection includes artifacts from all around the region, such as Ottoman pottery and jewelry crafted by ancient Bedouin tribes. There is also a library, a research center, and a variety of interactive exhibits in the museum.

Once, the Al Zubarah Fort in northwest Qatar operated as an important trade port for the region. The fort operated as a base for pearl fishing and trade until it was abandoned in the 18th century. Visitors may now explore the fort's halls as a museum to learn more about its history and current importance in the region.

The Qatari Heritage Village, a living museum devoted to Qatar's traditional culture and way of life, is located near Al Khor. In addition to traditional arts and crafts, the museum features a variety of replica buildings and exhibitions. Visitors may participate in courses, experience authentic Qatari hospitality, and learn about the country's history and culture.

The National Museum of Qatar is the largest in Qatar, and it is located in the capital. The museum's collection includes materials from all around the world, ranging from ancient fossils to modern works of art. The museum also has a research center, library, and a variety of interactive exhibits.

Qatar is home to some of the world's most spectacular and unusual museums. Each of these seven museums offers a unique and interesting glimpse into Qatar's broad cultural and historical background. These seven museums provide an incredible experience for all tourists, whether they are looking for an educational opportunity, a taste of traditional Qatari hospitality, or just a chance to learn about the country's art and culture.

Shopping

Qatar is a modest yet prosperous country in the Middle East. As a result, it has developed into a center for global trade, with a number of shopping centers that provide a wide range of products and services. The 10 most well-liked shopping centers in Qatar will be examined and their features, services, and facilities will be covered in this guide.

The Mall of Qatar, the biggest shopping mall in Qatar, is the first retail complex on our list. There are more than 500 shops there, including ones for multinational retailers like Zara, H&M, and Sephora. The mall also has a sizable entertainment complex with a bowling alley, a movie theater, and an ice rink. The mall also sponsors a variety of cultural activities, such as performances by artists from across the world.

The Villaggio Mall in the Aspire Zone is the second retail center on our list. This shopping center is well-known for its distinctive design, which was inspired by Italian canals and bridges. The mall is home to a wide range of retailers, from exclusive boutiques to fast-fashion chains. A sizable food court with a wide selection of foreign cuisine is also included.

The Doha Festival City, which is situated in the center of Qatar, is the third retail center on our list. From high-end brands to independent retailers, this mall offers a diverse selection of businesses. Together with an IMAX cinema and a bowling alley, it also has a sizable entertainment complex. A variety of activities, including live concerts and cultural acts, are also held in the mall.

The Lagoona Mall, which is situated in West Bay, is the fourth retail center on our list. From electronics stores to businesses selling designer goods, this mall has a broad variety of shops and services. A sizable food court with a wide selection of foreign cuisine is also included. A variety of activities, including live music performances and art exhibits, are also held in the mall.

The Landmark Mall, which can be found in the West Bay region, is the sixth retail center on our list. This mall has a lot of regional stores in addition to a selection of international brands. The mall also organizes a variety of cultural activities, such as performances by foreign artists.

The Al Khor Mall, which is situated in Qatar's north, is the sixth retail center on our list. From high-end brands to independent retailers, this mall offers a diverse selection of businesses. A sizable food court with a wide selection of foreign cuisine is also included. A variety of activities, including live concerts and cultural acts, are also held in the mall.

The City Center Mall, which lies in the center of Doha, is the eighth retail center on our list. From high-end brands to independent retailers, this mall offers a diverse selection of businesses. Together with an IMAX cinema and a bowling alley, it also has a sizable entertainment complex. A variety of activities, including live concerts and cultural acts, are also held in the mall.

The Ezdan Mall, which is situated in Al Wakra, is the eighth retail center on our list. From high-end brands to independent retailers, this mall offers a diverse selection of businesses. A sizable food court with a wide selection of foreign cuisine is also included. A variety of activities, including live music performances and art exhibits, are also held in the mall.

The Doha Mall, which is situated in the center of Qatar, is the ninth retail center on our list. From high-end brands to independent retailers, this mall offers a diverse selection of businesses. Together with an IMAX cinema and a bowling alley, it also has a sizable entertainment complex. A variety of activities, including live concerts and cultural acts, are also held in the mall.

Lastly, the Royal Plaza Mall, which is situated in the Al Sadd neighborhood, is the tenth retail center on our list. From high-end brands to independent retailers, this mall offers a diverse selection of businesses. A sizable food court with a wide selection of foreign cuisine is also included. A variety of activities, including live music performances and art exhibits, are also held in the mall.

Many shopping centers in Qatar provide a wide range of products and services. There is something for everyone, from the Royal Plaza Mall to the Mall of Qatar, which is the biggest mall in Qatar. Each shopping center provides a distinctive experience with a variety of shops, services, and cultural activities. Qatar includes both expensive brands and regional stores, so there is something for everyone.

CHAPTER SIX

Food And Drinks

Local Cuisines

The cuisine of Qatar, a rapidly expanding Middle Eastern country, reflects the region's diverse cultures and influences. Qatar's culinary landscape is a true melting pot of flavors, spanning from traditional Bedouin food to modern fusion cuisine. The best regional cuisine in Qatar is listed here for you to try on your next visit.

The traditional Bedouin meal, which consists mostly of kebabs and stews prepared from goat and sheep, comes first. Bedouin cuisine is tasty because it is cooked in a pit oven and uses a variety of herbs and spices. Machboos, a Bedouin dish consisting of fragrant rice cooked with meat, vegetables, and spices, merits particular note.

The next kind of cuisine is modern fusion, which is popular in Qatari cafés and restaurants. In this cuisine, traditional ingredients and flavors are mixed with cutting-edge procedures and presentation approaches to produce dishes that are both edible and visually beautiful. Popular fusion food includes shawarma wraps, mezze platters, and kofta kebabs.

The third benefit of Qatar's large coastline is the number of seafood dishes. Some of the area restaurants provide seafood, which might include anything from grilled prawns and lobster to steamed fish and calamari. A popular regional dish is machbous sahli, a fish stew cooked in a traditional clay pot and served with flatbread.

Qatar's traditional cuisine is concentrated mostly on rice, pork, and dairy dishes, ranking fourth. Qatari cuisine includes harees, a slow-cooked stew of meat and grains, kabsa, a fragrant rice dish cooked with spiced meat, and tharid, a tiered feast of meat, vegetables, and flatbread.

Yemeni cuisine, which is known for its spicy spices and quantity of fish, ranks fifth. Yemeni dishes include mandi, a slow-cooked rice dish with spiced meat, and saltah, a stew of vegetables, pig, and spices.

The sixth option is Indian cuisine, which is popular in Qatar due to the large Indian ex-pat community. Indian cuisine is often served with chapati bread and rice, and some of the most well-known dishes include tandoori chicken, curries, and biryani.

The use of fresh herbs, spices, and vegetables distinguishes Lebanese cuisine, which ranks eighth. Some of the most well-known Lebanese cuisines are hummus, tabouleh, falafel, and shawarma.

The eighth category is Turkish cuisine, which is notable for its abundance of grilled meats. Popular Turkish meals include kebabs, doner kebabs, and pide, a flatbread covered with meats, vegetables, and cheese.

The ninth category is Persian cuisine, which is characterized by the use of aromatic herbs and spices. Among the most famous Persian dishes are kabab torsh, a grilled kebab dish made with seasoned ground beef, and khoresht, a meat, vegetable, and spice stew.

Then there's the international cuisine available in many of Qatar's cafés and restaurants. This includes several foreign cuisines such as Italian, French, Chinese, Japanese, and Mexican.

Whichever cuisine you choose, there is sure to be something to entice your taste buds on Qatar's wide culinary scene. There will be something for you, whether you like traditional Bedouin food or a modern fusion meal. What are you still waiting for? Try one of these delectable regional delicacies on your next vacation to Qatar.

Local Drinks

Despite being a small, dry nation in the Middle East, Qatar produces some of the most remarkable and delectable drinks on the globe. The native drinks of the country provide a wide range of flavors and aromas, ranging from traditional Arabic coffee to fragrant herbal teas. These are the best regional drinks in Qatar that everyone should try at least once.

1. Arabic Coffee: This traditional Arab drink is made from a special blend of roasted and finely ground beans. The powder is served with a dash of saffron after being boiled with a small amount of cardamom. It has a particular flavor that is nutty and somewhat sweet.

2. Traditional qahwa is a drink made from ground green coffee beans, cardamom, and sometimes cinnamon. It may be drunk hot or cold and is often served with dates.

3. Laban: This is a common yogurt-based morning beverage. It is made by combining yogurt, water, salt, and a few spices. It has a sweet and tangy flavor and is surprisingly refreshing.

4. Qamar Al-Din: A famous drink made with sugar, orange blossom water, and dried apricots. It is often served cold and has a sweet, fruity flavor.

5. The popular tea known as karak is made with black tea, cardamom, and ginger. It has a little spicy flavor and is often served with milk and sugar on the side.

6. Sahlab: A thick beverage made with milk, sugar, and powdered orchid root. It has a sweet, creamy flavor and is often served cold.

7. Tamar (rosewater, sugar, and dates) is a traditional Indian sweet beverage. It has a characteristic sweet and floral flavor and is served cold.

8. Aseer Asab is traditionally made with sugar, rosewater, and lemon juice. It is often served cold and has a sweet, tangy flavor.

9. The delightful syrup known as jallab is made from dates, grape molasses, and rosewater. It's usually served with ice and tastes sweet and fruity.

10. Halab is a traditional beverage made from fermented wheat and barley. It has a

somewhat acidic flavor and is often served chilled.

Whichever drink you select, each of these regional drinks in Qatar will deliver an unforgettable experience. There is something for everyone in this broad blend, from sweet and fruity to acidic and sour. Why not try one (or more!) of these drinks?

Street Foods

Qatar, a Middle Eastern country, is known for its rich culture, active history, and, of course, exquisite street food. Street food, or "quick food," as it is colloquially known, is a convenient and cost-effective way to sample local cuisine. Excellent street food, ranging from classic Middle Eastern delights to inventive fusion cuisine, can be found across

Qatar. This is a list of the greatest street foods in Qatar that you must try:

1. Shawarma, a popular Middle Eastern street food, consists of thin slices of beef or chicken marinated in spices and cooked on a rotating spit. After that, it is served in a wrap or pita with a variety of toppings such as tahini, hummus, and pickled vegetables.

2. Falafel: Falafel is a popular vegetarian street dish in Qatar. It's made with ground chickpeas, herbs, and spices, then deep-fried and served in a pita or wrap with a variety of toppings.

3. Kebab: Kebab is a popular street dish in Qatar, consisting of spice-marinated beef and vegetable mince cooked on a skewer. It is

often served in a wrap or pita with a variety of sauces and toppings.

4. Manakish: Za'atar, a blend of herbs, spices, and olive oil, is a popular topping for flatbreads in this well-known Middle Eastern street food. Pickled veggies and hummus are usually served on the side.

5. Fatayer: A popular street meal in Qatar, fatayer is made with flatbread packed with minced beef or veggies and deep-fried. It's usually accompanied by pickled veggies and tahini on the side.

6. Lahoh: A popular street food in Qatar, lahoh is made with a dough that resembles a pancake and is filled with various ingredients such as minced beef or veggies before being topped with feta cheese and spices.

7. Umm Ali: Umm Ali is a well-known Middle Eastern delicacy made with a blend of nuts and dried fruits and baked in a thick custard.

8. A mix of vegetables, including cucumbers, tomatoes, and radishes, are combined with a lemon-sumac dressing to form fattoush, a popular Middle Eastern salad.

9. Hummus: Hummus is a popular Middle Eastern dip made with mashed chickpeas, olive oil, and tahini that are often served with pita bread or vegetables.

10. Zucchini are stuffed with ground beef, herbs, and spices before being cooked in a tomato-based sauce in the traditional Middle Eastern dish known as kousa. It is often served with rice.

Here are just a few examples of the delectable street food available in Qatar. Everyone will find something they like, whether they want a short snack or a large meal. If you ever visit Qatar, be sure to try some of these street delicacies!

CHAPTER SEVEN

Health And Safety

Vaccination

Vaccination is an important public health measure for preventing the spread of infectious diseases. Vaccination is a top goal for Qatar's Ministry of Public Health and an essential component of the country's healthcare system (MoPH). Measles, rubella, diphtheria, tetanus, and polio are just a handful of the vaccine-preventable diseases that people may be protected against.

The MoPH makes vaccinations such as the measles, mumps, rubella (MMR) vaccine, the polio vaccine, and the meningococcal vaccine available to the public. Vaccinations are free in Qatar, and the MoPH provides immunization services to both adults and children. Vaccinations are available in public health centers, private hospitals, and public hospitals.

The purpose of Qatar's vaccination program is to ensure that every child obtains the necessary vaccines within their first year of life. The government has also initiated a number of initiatives to educate the public about the need for immunizations. The purpose of these initiatives is to educate the public on the benefits of vaccination, diseases that it may prevent, and vaccine safety.

In addition to these public awareness campaigns, Qatar has implemented a number of efforts to ensure that vaccination rates remain high. These initiatives include compensating medical personnel who provide vaccines, making vaccinations available in pharmacies, and improving immunization availability in remote areas. The MoPH has also established a national immunization registry to monitor the progress of the nation's vaccination program.

The vaccination program in Qatar has been successful in increasing immunization rates and protecting the population from diseases that may be avoided with vaccines. The country has achieved outstanding vaccine coverage rates, with over 95% of children receiving the whole set of recommended immunizations by the age of two. As seen by the high percentage of coverage, the MoPH is dedicated to ensuring that all children and adults in Qatar are protected against diseases that may be avoided via immunization.

Dealing With Emergencies

Qatar is a small but fast-growing Middle Eastern country with a population of over three million people. The country is prone to both man-made disasters like civil unrest and industrial accidents, as well as natural disasters such as floods, earthquakes, and extreme heat. As a consequence, the government and other relevant entities must have a sound emergency response plan.

Qatar's government has made steps to safeguard its citizens from natural disasters. It has prepared an emergency response strategy to provide a complete response to any natural disaster. As part of this approach, a command center, an emergency hotline, and a rapid response team will be formed. The government has also invested in public awareness campaigns to educate people on how to avoid and cope with natural disasters.

Qatar has also taken proactive efforts to protect its citizens from man-made disasters. It has formed a dedicated security force and invested in cutting-edge security technology to protect critical infrastructure. In addition, the government has established a network of evacuation routes and emergency shelters. In addition to providing a venue for medical care and other assistance, these organizations provide a haven for those affected by disasters.

In addition to these proactive steps, Qatar has implemented preventative measures to help avoid problems before they occur. This includes enforcing workplace safety regulations and keeping a watch out for potential hazards at industrial sites. The government has also enacted a slew of laws and regulations to protect inhabitants from exploitation or abuse.

When it comes to dealing with crises, Qatar has implemented several steps to ensure the safety and security of its citizens. The government has shown its commitment to safeguarding the safety of its citizens by investing in a comprehensive disaster response plan, implementing preventative measures, and providing assistance to those affected.

Conclusion

Qatar is a fascinating and diverse tourism destination with enough to offer all types of visitors. From its rich cultural past to its world-class attractions, there is something for everyone. Qatar has something for everyone, whether they want a luxurious holiday, a weekend of adventure, or an opportunity to learn about the region's unique cultures.

Qatar is an excellent location for travelers of all interests and backgrounds due to its cutting-edge infrastructure, thriving tourism industry, and safe environment. Qatar offers something for everyone, whether you're looking for a cultural experience, a chance to explore the region's natural wonders, or a luxurious escape.

Therefore, don't put it off any longer and start planning your trip to Qatar right now!

Printed in Great Britain
by Amazon